Fly Fishing
MADE EASY

Published by Hyndman Publishing, PO Box 5017, Dunedin
ISBN 1-877168-68-8

TEXT: © Mike Weddell
DESIGN & ARTWORK: Dileva Design Ltd
PRINTING: Tablet Colour Print

All rights reserved. No part of this publication is to be produced, stored in a retrieval system, or transmitted in any form or by means electronic, mechanical, or photocopying without prior written permission of the publisher.

Contents

- 4 Introduction
- 6 **Tackle & Knots**
- 7 The Rod
- 9 The Reel
- 9 The Line
- 12 The Leader
- 14 Other Items of Tackle
- 15 Knots
- 19 **Casting**
- 20 Casting Techniques
- 26 Retrieving the Line
- 28 **Catching Techniques**
- 28 The Strike
- 28 Playing Fish
- 29 Netting Fish
- 29 Returning Fish
- 30 **Trout – The Need to Understand Them**
- 31 Vision
- 33 Hearing
- 34 Feeding
- 35 **Trout Food**
- 35 Rivers and Streams
- 38 Stillwaters
- 41 **Choosing the Right Fly**
- 44 Sample Fly Selection
- 49 **Fishing Streams & Rivers**
- 54 **Fishing Stillwaters**
- 58 **Learning Tips**
- 62 Keeping a Fishing Diary

Introduction

Fly fishing can be approached in many different ways. At one end of the spectrum any old fly is chosen, tied on and cast on the water in the hope that a trout will take hold. At the opposite end of the spectrum every conceivable factor is taken into account: the season of the year; the time of day; the height of the water; what the trout may be feeding on; and at what depth and position in the pool they are lying. Most fly fishers probably operate somewhere in the middle, but as in all activities the more thought put in and the more knowledge a fly fisher has, the better the chance of success.

In this book we will look at the factors that affect the fly fisher's ability to catch trout and how to adapt our approach to allow for them. There is one factor that the book cannot help with and that is experience – that is up to you to gain by fishing as much as possible, a delightful challenge.

Tackle
and Knots

To the beginner the array of tackle available to the fly fisher is mind-boggling and this is probably the first obstacle to overcome when taking up fly fishing. There are a few basic items necessary for fly fishing: rod, reel, line, leader and fly. Of these items the fly is the most difficult to deal with and deserves a chapter on its own, (see pages 41–47). Here we will deal with the other four.

In an ideal world it is the size of the fly that determines the thickness of the leader, which in turn determines the weight of line used and therefore the strength of the rod. We don't live in an ideal world and most of us will buy one rod to cover all our fly fishing. Thus the rod we choose will need to match the size of the fly we will fish most of the time, and the reel, line and leader will follow.

THE ROD

Rods are rated according to the line weight they will cast and both lines and rods are marked with a number to make it easy to match them.

If most of your fishing will be done with feathered lures tied on size 8 hooks or bigger, then a rod taking an 8, 9 or 10 weight line will be best suited to the purpose. If most of your fishing will be done with flies of size 10 to 16, then your best match is a rod of 5, 6 or 7 weight. If you fish really small flies a lot of the time (size 16 or less) then an even lighter rod would be indicated, but for most New Zealand fishing size 5 is as light as we need to go.

If the water you fish regularly has baitfish as the dominant trout food, then the heavier outfit would be more appropriate. If the fishery is dominated by insect-feeding fish however, the lighter outfit would be more applicable.

Once we have decided on the weight of rod we need, length is the next factor to consider. Many fly fishers erroneously think that the longer the rod, the further they can cast with it. This is not true because a very long rod puts us at a great mechanical disadvantage and it takes a lot of strength to use it. Most types of New Zealand fishing can be covered by rods in the 2.5 – 3 metre range.

One important factor when deciding on a suitable rod length is the type of water to be fished. Small waters surrounded by trees are more easily fished with a short rod whereas large waters such as lakes or big rivers are more suited to longer rods. A good average length to cover most fishing is about 2.7 metres.

There are several different materials used in the manufacture of rods but for all practical purposes rods made from carbon fibre (graphite) are the most suitable for the beginner. Carbon fibre is very light and durable. Rods made from this material vary in price, from the cheap to the astronomically expensive. Cheap to the middle of the range is probably best for beginners – expensive rods would only be a worry to use in case of breakage. There are very good rods made here in New Zealand and they are at least as good as any brought in from overseas.

Until fairly recently 2 piece rods were the norm but multi piece rods are becoming more common. Three and more piece rods are easier to transport than two piece models, but are slightly more expensive. While fishing they are virtually indistinguishable from each other.

> *It is a good idea to store your rod in a carrying tube when not actually fishing to avoid damage.*

We now come to that rather nebulous factor – rod action. Rod actions vary from 'all through' to fast. By far the easiest action to learn to cast with is what would be classed as medium action. This means that the rod flexes through about two thirds of its length when casting 10 metres of matching line. An 'all through' action rod feels as if it is bending in the handle under your hand and a fast action rod feels as if only the tip is flexing.

> *Remember that when buying a rod you are not buying the skill to use it – a cheap rod in skilful hands works better than an expensive rod used without skill. Rods are often better than the fly fishers using them.*

If you eventually feel that your skill has reached a level where a better rod is warranted, try lots of different rods – the one that feels best is the one that's best for you. Don't get rid of the old rod; keep it as a spare. If you travel a couple of hours to your fishing destination and break a rod in the first hour or so, your day is finished unless you have a spare rod.

TACKLE & KNOTS

> *Just a word on maintenance: it's a good idea to wax the joints of your rod. Rubbing them with wax will stop the joints wearing and the section throwing off while casting.*

THE REEL

Fly reels are simple affairs. They need to hold the fly line to be used and enough backing to suit the kind of fishing to be done. The reel should be as light as possible while being strong enough to withstand the knocks of constant use. The drum and frame should have no large gaps between them where the line can jam. The mechanism should be simple so there is less that can go wrong. Many modern reels boast disc drags (at a cost), but even the hardest running trout can be handled with a simple check mechanism. Any extra pressure can be applied by hand by pressing a finger on the rim of the reel.

To facilitate rapid recovery of the line while winding in it is better to have a narrow, large diameter reel than a wide, small diameter model. The large diameter will retrieve more line per turn of the handle.

A good quality fly reel should last 30 years or more of constant use and it pays not to go for the cheapest available. It is also a good idea to go for a model for which spare spools are available, so that you can carry an alternative line without the expense of having to buy a separate reel for it.

> *Be sure to keep the reel clean and lightly oiled.*

THE LINE

There is a vast array of fly lines available, with different tapers, different densities and different colours in all sorts of combinations. This variety can be very confusing, even for relatively experienced fly fishers.

The type of fishing that you do will determine the line needed. If you wish to fish a fly close to or on the surface a floating line is a must. Sinking lines are used to get the fly down to the required depth (usually close to the bottom). The rate of sink required will be determined by the depth of the water and the speed of the current. In deep water with a fast current a fast sink line is necessary to get near the bottom. A line of lower density can be used in shallower or slower water.

The most versatile line is the floater. Flies can be fished on, just below or well below the surface with a floater by adjusting the length of the leader and the weight of the fly. Unless most of your fishing is done with large feathered lures, a floating line will be the line of choice.

Once the density of line has been settled on there is the taper to consider. There are three basic tapers of line available: double taper, weight forward and shooting taper. Each has its advantages and disadvantages.

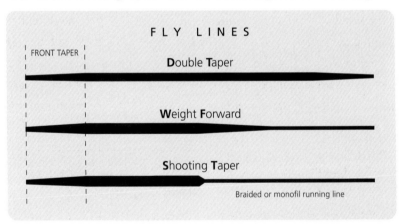

Double Taper

This line has an identical short taper to a fine tip at each end. The advantages of this line are you can lift as much line off the water as your casting technique/rod combination will allow, and when one end wears out you can turn it around and effectively have a new line. The disadvantages are it is bulkier than the other lines and needs a bigger reel to hold it, and it doesn't shoot as well.

Weight Forward

The weight forward line is essentially the front ten or so metres of a double taper with the rest of it being made up of thin running line. The shape of the line allows it to shoot better and it takes up less room on the reel. The disadvantages are that the line must be pulled in until the back of the thick part is at or near the tip ring of the rod before it can be cast. Also there is a tendency for it to wear on the running line immediately behind the head. Once any part of the line is too worn to be used it must be discarded as it can't be turned around like the double taper.

Shooting Taper

This is the line of choice for casting long distances when combined with good casting technique. The very thin running line (usually nylon, either braided or monofil) allows a much longer shoot to be made. In a sinking version it gets down faster than the other types of lines. A major disadvantage is the difficulty in controlling the fine running line as it is prone to tangling. This line is similar to the weight forward in that the head must be at or near the tip ring to enable a cast to be made.

> **LINE COLOUR** *There is much debate about line colour, especially that of floating lines. Some argue that brightly coloured lines scare fish, but since fish observe floating lines from beneath, they are looking against the light and see only a silhouette. And the fly line should not pass over a fish - ideally only a small part of the leader tippet gets near a fish. Without doubt it is much easier to fish with a line that is brightly coloured - the bright colour helps us see what the line is doing and watching the tip of the line lets us know when a fish has taken the fly. I used a bright orange line throughout my most successful season.*

THE LEADER

The leader is the tapered link between the line and the fly (or flies) and is made of nylon or similar monofil materials. There are also some leaders that have a braided section next to the fly line. The braid does not coil up when pulled from the reel as monofil tends to do.

The thin end of the leader to which the fly is attached is called the tippet. This can be part of a continuous leader or added according to the thickness required. A good method is to buy a leader with the heaviest tippet you are likely to need. If a finer tippet is required just knot on a short piece of nylon to suit. Generally speaking, the larger and heavier the fly, the thicker the tippet should be.

The overall length of the leader is determined by casting proficiency and how close the fly is fished to the surface. A very short leader can be used and even be an advantage when fishing with a sinking line, as this pulls the fly down quickly with the line. A long leader in this case would leave the fly behind, higher in the water.

A long leader is necessary when fishing a fly at or near the surface in clear water, and also when using a floating line to fish a nymph close to the bottom.

> *Regular leader tangles suggest poor casting technique or too long a leader. If shortening the leader doesn't work, get in some casting practice. It is also a good idea to reduce the length of leader if it is windy. Usually shortening the tippet is all that is necessary to achieve this.*

If you wish to fish more than one fly (regulations permitting), this can be achieved by either tying another piece of nylon to the bend of the first fly,

The complete story; rod, fishing vest and trout!

TACKLE & KNOTS

then adding another fly to the end of that, or by tying a dropper on the leader. The dropper is a short piece of nylon sticking out from the leader the desired distance above the end fly.

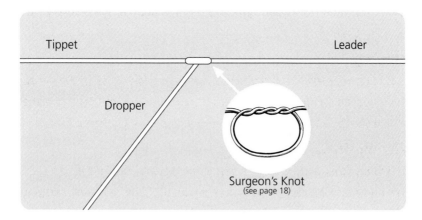

Tippet Material
We need to carry spools of spare tippet material of varying diameters and breaking strains, as we may need a finer tippet. You'll also find that when you change flies the tippet gets shorter and eventually needs replacing.

OTHER ITEMS OF TACKLE
There are several other items of tackle which, while not strictly essential, can make things easier.

Fly Box
Any old container can be used to carry flies but it makes life a lot easier to use a box that keeps them in an orderly fashion so that a chosen pattern can be found quickly when the need arises.

Line snips
These should be kept handy at all times for cutting off flies and trimming knots.

Polarising Glasses

These could almost be classed as essential items. They cut the glare from the water, allowing you to see into it and to see your fly on the water. Eye protection from hooks and ultraviolet light is another good reason for wearing them.

Landing Net

A landing net makes it quicker and easier to get a trout out of the water. This is especially important if the fish is to be returned. Make sure the model chosen isn't clumsy to carry around and is easy to use.

Fishing Vest

The great advantage of using a vest is that all your tackle can be stored in it and when you pick it up along with your rod tube you know that you have everything you need for a day on the water. There is nothing more frustrating for the angler than arriving at the water and finding that some essential item of equipment is missing.

Strike indicator

Strike indicators are small, brightly coloured pieces of material, resembling Christmas decorations, that are attached to the leader to help identify when a trout takes a submerged fly. They come in various colours and materials, including yarn, polystyrene and plastic sheeting.

KNOTS

There are thousands of knots to choose from, but a few that are reliable and easy to tie are all that are needed. There is one to attach the leader to the fly line, one to attach tippet to leader and one to fasten the fly to the tippet.

Needle Knot

This is a knot that you shouldn't need to tie too often and rarely on the riverbank. When it is tied properly the leader should remain attached to

The one that didn't get away!

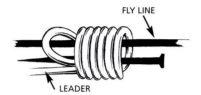

NEEDLE KNOT
FLY LINE
LEADER

the line until you think a new one is needed. The diagram is self explanatory but it helps if the turns are kept in place between finger and thumb as the knot is tightened for a neat finish.

Surgeon's Knot

This is a quick, simple, easy to tie knot that is strong and reliable. The tag hanging down towards the tippet can be used as a dropper. It is important to pull the knot up evenly on all four ends for the strongest possible result. Three turns are needed for fine tippets but for thicker nylon two will suffice.

SURGEON'S KNOT
LEADER
TIPPET

Blood Knot

This too is a strong, reliable knot but only if it is tied well – many anglers fail to tie this knot correctly. The correct way to tie it is to use at least six but no more than eight turns, draw it up slowly by pulling on the tippet, pull on the tag to be cut off, then pull on the tippet again before trimming off the tag end.

If you think you need to wet knots before you tighten them and you can't be convinced otherwise, do so. Equally if you tuck the tag of the blood knot and you think it worthwhile, do so. (Both in fact are a waste of time.)

It is also worth practising your knots so that you can tie them quickly and reliably. You will need to be able to tie them under pressure on the water, when it may be cold, the wind blowing, light poor and trout rising all around.

BLOOD KNOT

Casting

In fly fishing casting is of the utmost importance. You will often hear it said that you don't need to be a good caster to catch fish. This may be true some of the time, but if you want to be a good fly fisher – one that can catch fish in most places and under less than perfect conditions – then you need to cast well.

It is pointless buying good tackle, expertly tied flies, and fishing in some of the best waters in the world, if you can't put a fly where you want it in the correct way most of the time. Blaming the wind, long grass or high banks for casts that go wrong is a waste of time. Trout won't take pity on a pathetic caster by making themselves easy to catch. You should decide now that you are going to practise casting until you are proficient enough to fish in most conditions.

Now that you have decided to improve your casting you need to practise, but practice itself is not enough – you need to practise the right things. What follows is the way to go about it.

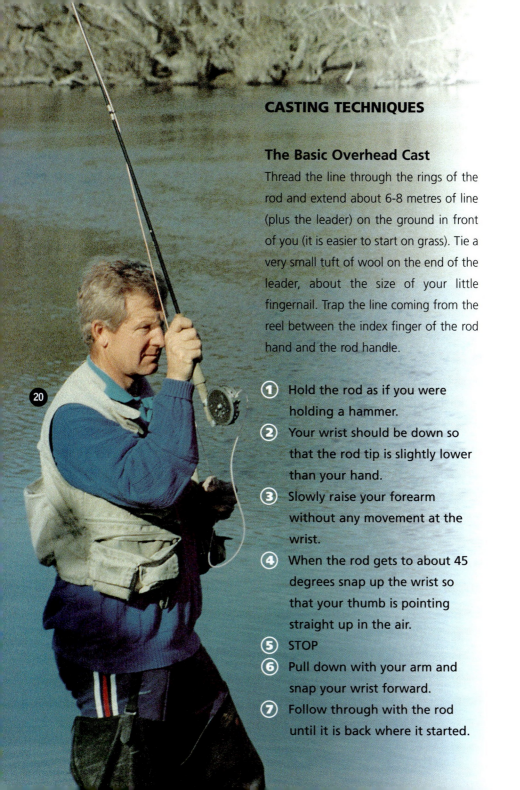

CASTING TECHNIQUES

The Basic Overhead Cast

Thread the line through the rings of the rod and extend about 6-8 metres of line (plus the leader) on the ground in front of you (it is easier to start on grass). Tie a very small tuft of wool on the end of the leader, about the size of your little fingernail. Trap the line coming from the reel between the index finger of the rod hand and the rod handle.

1. Hold the rod as if you were holding a hammer.
2. Your wrist should be down so that the rod tip is slightly lower than your hand.
3. Slowly raise your forearm without any movement at the wrist.
4. When the rod gets to about 45 degrees snap up the wrist so that your thumb is pointing straight up in the air.
5. STOP
6. Pull down with your arm and snap your wrist forward.
7. Follow through with the rod until it is back where it started.

CASTING

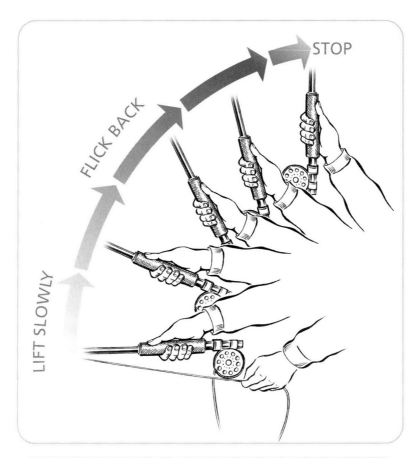

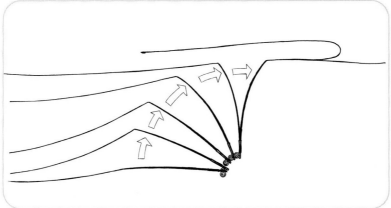

CASTING

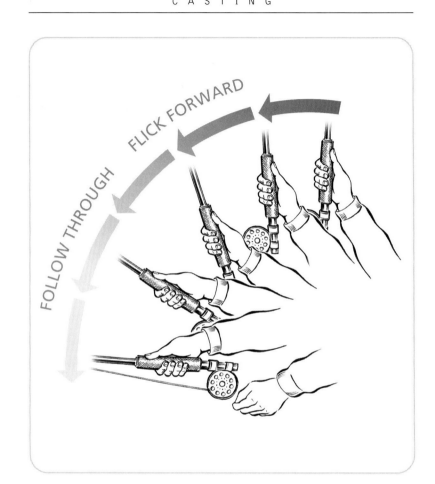

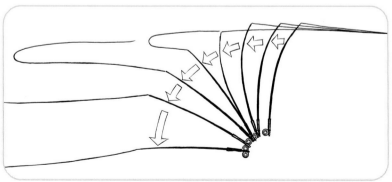

There are several common mistakes that should be avoided. Don't just cast with the wrist; make sure the arm starts the movement. The hand actually moves from waist level to face level and back again during the cast. Most of the effort involved in casting is on the back cast – in fact, it is easier to think of it as an up cast rather than a back cast. On the forward cast flick forward and follow through. Don't push, as this stops the line straightening. If the line goes up in the air in front and then dribbles in coils onto the grass, you have taken the rod too far back on the back cast.

When practising make one cast at a time; don't run one cast into another. Pause between casts and make sure the rod is in the correct position to start the next cast. Only practise for 10 minutes at a time, as it is hard to concentrate for long spells. Remember, if the line doesn't extend properly it isn't the rod's fault – it's yours, and you'll need to change something to make it better.

When casting on water for the first time it is easier to cast downstream, as the current keeps the line straight.

Use of the Line Hand

The hand that holds the rod controls the cast, but the other hand is just as important as it controls the line. It controls the shoot and retrieve of the line and can be used to pull on the line to increase its speed. For the basic cast in which you are just lifting off and recasting a fixed length of line, the line hand does very little. Hold the line between forefinger and thumb with a loop of slack line between the reel and line hand. This stops the line hand resisting the movement of the rod hand during the cast. The line hand should be held still with the elbow slightly bent throughout the cast. The line hand should not follow the rod hand.

The False Cast

False casting is casting the line back and forward in the air without allowing it to touch the water. The first part, getting the line off the water and into the air, is the same as the basic cast. The difference comes on the forward part. The downward movement of the arm is eliminated; immediately after the STOP (see page 20) the wrist is snapped forward but there is no follow through. As soon as the line has extended forward in the air the wrist is snapped back again to cast the line to the rear. This can be continued indefinitely until you want to put the line back on the water. However, it is a good idea to keep false casts to a minimum as if anything is going to go wrong it usually happens while false casting.

FALSE CAST

Why do we need to false cast anyway? There are several reasons for false casting. The line can be extended in the air by shooting a little line on each cast. Casting back and forward in the air is also used for ridding a dry fly of water so that it will float when dropped onto the water again. Most fly fishers make too many false casts: 3 should be the maximum. Remember, you can't catch fish with the fly whizzing back and forward in the air.

Shooting Line

Shooting line is a way of extending the line without having to make lots of false casts to attain a desired distance. A length of slack line is pulled from the reel and hangs between the reel and where it is held by the line hand. A normal cast is made and when the rod is horizontal the line hand releases its hold on the line. The momentum of the line extended beyond the rod tip pulls the loose line out through the rings.

If the line hand releases the line too early the line will pile up on the water. It is better to release too late rather than too early. The correct timing of the release is immediately after the wrist snap of the rod hand on the forward cast.

> With practice it is possible to shoot ten or more metres of line, but it is best to practise shooting 1 or 2 metres to start with.

The Single Haul

The single haul is one way of lifting a longer line from the water without having to pull it in and then shoot it out again. Pull down on the line with the line hand as the back cast is made. This increases the flex in the rod and makes the line travel faster, ensuring that the whole length will straighten to the rear before the forward cast is commenced.

If ultimate distance is your aim there is also a double haul, which involves another pull on the line during the forward cast. The timing of this is critical however, and the basic cast needs to be perfected before it is worth learning the double haul.

It is a mistake to strive for distance. It's better to cast a short but well controlled line than a messy long one. Most fish are probably caught at a range of less than 10 metres on all but the biggest of waters. However, it is never a disadvantage to be able to cast a long way even if you are never called upon to do so. If you can cast 20 metres but usually fish at 10–12 metres, then it will feel easy and you are much less likely to make mistakes. If your maximum distance is 12 metres and you are fishing at that range, you are on the brink of disaster all of the time. There will be more hook ups on the bank behind, more tangled leaders and more splashy casts that scare the fish. Taking out tangles and retrieving flies from bankside vegetation wastes fishing time. Always fish at a comfortable distance.

Getting Started

One problem that beginners encounter is how to get started with a cast – in other words, how to get enough line out to make the rod work. Thread the line and leader through the rod rings (it is easier to double over part of the fly line to do this rather than using the thin end of the leader), then tie on the fly. Flick the length of leader and line that is beyond the rod tip onto the water. Keeping the rod tip close to the water, pull a metre or so of line from the reel and move the rod sharply to one side, keeping the tip low. This will pull the line out through the rings. Repeat this several times until there is enough line out to cast. On flowing water the line will be carried away downstream and straighten; on stillwater the wind may help drift the line out. If there is no wind, walk along the bank a few paces, letting the slack line pull out as you go.

RETRIEVING THE LINE

The line is retrieved either to allow another cast to be made; to keep contact with the fly when it is drifting; or to move the fly through the water in a particular way. There are two main ways of retrieving line: you can pull the line in and gather it in loops in the line hand or drop to the ground (loop retrieving – see illustration left), or gather it in coils in the palm of the line hand (figure of eight retrieve – see illustrations opposite). The former allows a fast retrieve, whereas the latter can only be done slowly. The looping method allows the fly to be retrieved in short spurts, while the coiling method allows a more continuous retrieve.

◀ **LOOP RETRIEVE**
The line is held in loops between the forefinger and thumb in order of retrieval.

CASTING

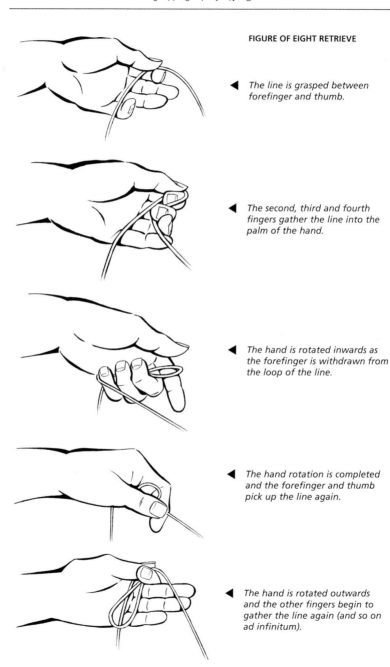

FIGURE OF EIGHT RETRIEVE

◀ The line is grasped between forefinger and thumb.

◀ The second, third and fourth fingers gather the line into the palm of the hand.

◀ The hand is rotated inwards as the forefinger is withdrawn from the loop of the line.

◀ The hand rotation is completed and the forefinger and thumb pick up the line again.

◀ The hand is rotated outwards and the other fingers begin to gather the line again (and so on ad infinitum).

Catching techniques

THE STRIKE

The term 'strike' suggests a strong movement – a better way to think of it is tightening onto the fish. The rod should be raised till the butt is vertical and the weight of the fish is felt. Any sharp, jerky movement should be avoided as this could lead to a break off, especially when using a light tippet.

PLAYING FISH

The rules about playing fish are simple: keep a steady pressure on the fish by keeping the rod up (somewhere between 45 and 90 degrees), and don't let the line go slack. If you have slack line between your hand and the reel, let it out if the fish runs away from you, or pull it in by hand if the fish runs towards you. It is just as easy to play a fish this way as it is to play it from the reel. For most beginners the thing to remember is not to take too long to play out a fish; it should rarely take more than 5 minutes to land even quite large fish.

CATCHING TECHNIQUES

NETTING FISH

Generally the quickest way to get a fish out of the water is to net it. The best way to net a fish is to place the net in the water, draw the fish over it and then lift the net. Moving the net about in the water spooks the fish so keep it still.

Hold the fish in the net to remove the hook. Hold the trout so that it is lying on its back – this way it won't kick and it will be easier to get the hook out.

How to net your fish.

RETURNING FISH

This may seem rather optimistic, but of course fishing is an optimist's sport! If you wish to return fish they should be played out and returned to the water as quickly as possible. The critical part of the operation is the time the fish is kept out of the water – it should be less than 30 seconds. When the fish is placed back in the water hold it upright until it is able to swim away. If the fish keels over turn it upright again or it will not survive.

The correct way to release a trout.

Now we have a good idea of the basic equipment and techniques used in fly fishing. We can assemble our tackle, put the fly where we want it (most of the time), control the line, play the trout and (if we are so inclined) release it correctly afterwards. To really make the most of this knowledge, however, we need to learn more about the fish we are hoping to catch.

Trout
– the need to understand them

A great step in the direction of becoming a successful angler is accepting that the fish call the shots, and this is just as true in fly fishing as in any other sort of angling. To help us in our quest to catch trout it is a big advantage to know at least some of the shots that they will call. The more we know about trout the better our chances of catching them.

Trout, much like humans, want to get as much to eat as possible while expending as little energy as possible. This single factor governs what trout will feed on and where they will feed at any given time.

Trout are territorial and tend to inhabit certain parts of rivers or lakes for long periods. Brown trout will live in a particular area for years at a time, whereas rainbows may spend up to a season in one location. The territory must exhibit certain characteristics if the trout are to remain there. Well oxygenated water is vital, of course, but that is not all. There needs to be a supply of food, good feeding positions, and a safe haven to take refuge in when threatened.

Good feeding positions in running water are where the current

TROUT — the need to understand them

concentrates a stream of food past a position where a trout can lie sheltered from the current. When a food item drifts past, the fish moves out into the current and takes it, then moves back into slack water. In stillwaters trout must swim to find food and tend to have a regular beat which they patrol. In stillwaters concentrations of food occur around weedbeds or stream mouths.

Safe havens in a stream are beneath boulders or undercut banks, under trees or in deep water. In stillwaters weedbeds and deep water provide refuge.

This knowledge immediately suggests places that trout can be found — for example, along the edges of ripples in streams and around weedbeds in stillwaters. However, knowing where trout are to be found and being able to catch them are not the same thing. Trout are wild creatures and their instincts have evolved to help them survive. Understanding the defences of trout will help us overcome them.

VISION

Trout have good eyesight, with colour vision and the ability to see fairly fine detail. Their field of vision is important to the trout fisher. Trout cannot see immediately below them in the normal swimming position. This tells us that trout will take items of food that are level with, or above them, in the water. This means that our fly must be fished at the correct depth if it is to be seen by the trout.

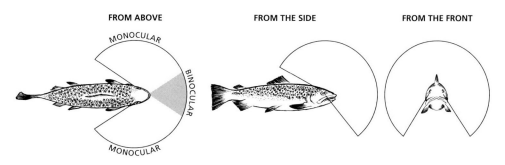

TROUT – the need to understand them

Of course trout do feed off the bottom, especially in stillwaters, and it is easy to tell when they are doing this, as they swim tail up and nose down so they can see the bottom close in front of them.

Trout have binocular vision immediately in front of them and monocular vision on both sides. They can see to the rear but have a small blind spot behind and below. This tells us that it is usually best to approach a trout from behind, as this avoids spooking it.

A cautious approach to a rising fish.

Unlike the human eye, the pupil of the trout's eye cannot dilate or contract to accommodate the amount of light shining on it. This means that trout don't see so well in bright sunlight, as they are dazzled, but see very well in overcast conditions. This explains why in bright sunlight it is often very easy to approach trout, while in overcast conditions they can be very difficult to catch.

The eyes of trout are well adapted to feeding in the dark. They can see things close to and above them, but very little at a distance. Of course this means that night fishing is an ideal approach to catching trout, but it is a good idea to perfect your technique in daylight before testing it in the dark.

Trout are very good at detecting movement, so if you can see a trout always assume that it can see you and if you have to move, move slowly. If you are on the skyline it is easier for trout to see you, so keep off the skyline.

You can use cover to approach trout, and cover behind is just as useful as cover in front. Cover behind, while you can still be seen, makes you much less obvious, while cover in front can keep you out of sight altogether.

HEARING

Most children that go fishing with adults think that trout can hear human voices, as they are told to keep quiet for fear of scaring the fish. If trout can hear human voices it doesn't seem to worry them too much, but there are sounds that scare them. What we call sound is the air vibrating – trout 'hearing' detects vibrations in the water. They can detect vibrations from heavy footfalls on the bank, the crunching of gravel or rocks knocking together. Trout seem to detect sounds better in flat water than in ripples, as the background noise of a ripple appears to mask other sounds.

Good cover for the angler here.

FEEDING

As we have already seen, trout need to feed efficiently, avoiding swimming against the current, but close enough to it to benefit from the passing food. The size of the food item plays a part in how far trout will swim for it. A large item such as a small fish or a cicada is worth swimming some distance for, but a midge or willow grub is not. This means that small flies have a better chance of being taken if they are close to the fish. The same applies in stillwaters – a trout will deviate more from its beat to take a large item of food than a small one.

Trout food

In general terms trout live in cool, well oxygenated water wherever they are found in the world; this is the habitat to which they have adapted. The same is true of the creatures that trout feed on. Consequently there is a great similarity in the diet of trout wherever they are found. There is, however, one major factor that determines the diet of trout and that is whether they live in flowing waters or stillwaters. To a lesser extent the variety of food items available to trout is also governed by the creatures that may be blown onto the water from the surrounding countryside.

RIVERS AND STREAMS

The commonest creatures that trout feed on in running waters are sedges and mayflies, but the snails, midges and stoneflies that live there also find their way into trout's stomachs. Beetles, cicadas, daddy longlegs, willow grubs and blowflies will be blown onto the water and taken by trout at times. In tidal waters small fish in the form of smelt or whitebait can form an important part of the trout diet.

Sedges

Sedges are related to moths and look very similar when flying. However, sedges are an aquatic insect and both the larval and pupal stages live in the water. There are cased larvae, sandy cased, horn cased and many others, as well as caseless larvae. Both the cased and caseless larvae are taken by trout; so too are the pupae and adults.

Larvae tend to live on the river bed on rocks and stones. They occasionally drift in the current, which is when trout feed on them.

The pupa swims towards the surface of the water where it hatches into an adult. The hatch usually occurs around dusk and on into darkness. Once hatched the adults run across the water to the riverbank and then fly off into the surrounding vegetation. Again during the hours of dusk and darkness they return to mate and lay their eggs. Trout feed on them on all of these occasions.

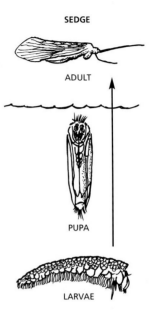

Mayflies

The mayfly has three stages to its life: nymph, dun and spinner. Nymphs live on stones on the riverbed and drift in the current. They swim to the surface to hatch into a dun. The Dun flies off the water and then moults, returning to the water as a spinner to mate and lay eggs. The spinner dies on laying its eggs and drifts down the river. All these stages are fed on by trout.

Mayflies hatch in the middle of the day

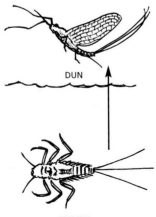

during the cooler parts of the year and around dawn and dusk in warm weather. Spinners return to the water when it is calm, which is often around dawn and dusk.

Stoneflies

Stoneflies are much more restricted in their range than sedges or mayflies and are usually found in colder, more bouldery waters. Stoneflies are a reliable indicator of good water quality. The nymphs live on stones and boulders and swim to the surface to hatch. In other countries trout feed on the adults immediately after hatching, but it is the nymph that is more commonly found in the stomachs of trout in New Zealand.

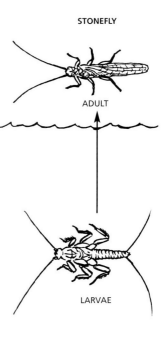

Midges

Midges are a creature of still or slow moving water, so are found away from the main current in flowing waters. The larvae live in silt so you can expect them to hatch near any silty areas in a river. These larvae are often bright red and are called bloodworms. Although they mainly live in the silt, they also swim around. The pupae swim to the surface to hatch out and are intercepted by trout. The hatches mainly occur around dusk and on into darkness and early in the morning. The adult midge is not as important as a trout food.

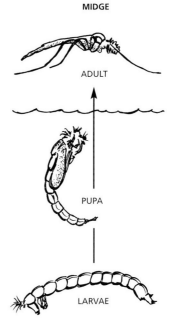

Snails

Snails can be found in great numbers in the slower moving parts of rivers. They are available to trout all of the time, as they live on top of whatever forms the riverbed and in weedbeds.

Terrestrial Insects

When the weather is warm there are a host of insects that are active and get blown onto the water. Terrestrials can make up a large percentage of the food available to trout in less fertile waters, such as high country streams. Brown beetles are usually the first terrestrials to appear in numbers in late spring, followed by green beetles in early and midsummer. Cicadas appear in summer, followed by daddy longlegs in autumn. Willow grubs drop onto the water throughout the summer, especially on warm days.

Baitfish

Baitfish play a small but significant part in the diet of river trout. Smelt and whitebait are usually present in large numbers when they appear in the tidal reaches of rivers. Trout will gorge on them and put on a lot of weight in a very short time. Late winter and early spring is the time for this feeding frenzy.

There are many other creatures that river trout feed on in the course of a year, but those I have covered here account for over 90% of the food taken by trout.

STILLWATERS

Some of the items of trout food found in flowing waters are also found in stillwaters (for example, midges, snails, sedges and terrestrials), but there are others that are found primarily in lakes and ponds. Waterboatmen, diving beetles, dragonflies and damselflies are common in stillwaters and fed upon by trout. In some lakes baitfish form the foundation of the trout fishery.

Waterboatmen

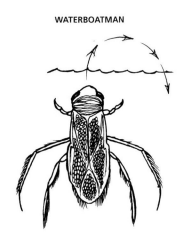

WATERBOATMAN

This insect lives underwater but breathes air and makes regular trips to the surface to breathe. It has wings and will occasionally fly. Trout intercept it going up to or coming down from the surface, or when it crashes onto the water post flight.

Diving Beetles

These shiny blackish beetles are about the size of a little fingernail. They breathe air and can fly like a waterboatman. Their larvae too can be found in trout. They look like a caseless caddis and are often mistaken for them. The larvae swim about and are easy pickings.

Dragonflies

The dragonfly nymph lives in silt on the bed of stillwaters. It hides in the silt and ambushes its prey, but does swim around and it then becomes the prey of trout. The nymphs migrate to shore to hatch and crawl out onto stones or up rushes before breaking out of the nymphal shuck. The adults too are taken by trout when they alight on the water.

Damselflies

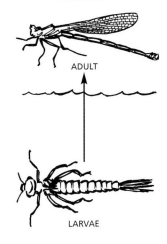

DAMSELFLY

ADULT

LARVAE

These creatures are closely related to dragonflies and are often erroneously given that name. The nymph, however, is quite different, as it is very active and swims about most of the time. It is long and thin, unlike the thickset dragonfly nymph.

The adult too is different, being smaller and finer than the dragonfly. The main difference is that the adult damselfly folds its wings along its back when it settles, whereas the dragonfly keeps its wings extended at 90 degrees to its body.

Damsel nymphs also crawl out of the water to hatch. There are many more damsels than dragons so they are more commonly found in trout. Trout often jump out of the water to take damselflies as they hover above the water.

Baitfish

In many North Island lakes (and to a lesser extent in some South Island lakes) baitfish form an important part of the diet of trout. At certain times of the year these small fish move into shallow water to spawn or gather at river mouths during migration, and this can attract large numbers of trout. Smelt are more important in the North Island, while landlocked whitebait and upland bullies feature more in the South.

Now that we are familiar with the main items on the trout's menu, we need to look at the imitations that we hope will catch them.

Insect life in a back country stream.

Choosing the right *Fly*

There is a bewildering array of flies available to the fly fisher; thousands of them, in fact. How can this be when trout feed on relatively few creatures? Well, over the years new patterns have been invented by different fly fishers in different places. However, many of these flies imitate the same creatures (the creatures being imitated are referred to here as 'naturals'). Once this is realised it makes the task of choosing the right fly easier. Things can be made easier still by carrying one good imitation for each of the creatures trout feed on in the waters you fish regularly.

> *Much has been written in fly fishing literature about the difference between dry fly and wet fly. Trout, however, do not think in those terms and neither should we: trout food is either under the water, in the surface film, or floating on the surface.*

If you can see what the trout are feeding on (for instance, mayfly duns or cicadas are easily seen floating on the surface of the water), then choosing the correct imitation is even easier. But choosing the correct imitation from your fly box is only half the battle. It may look natural to you, but from the trout's point of view it has to not only look like the real thing, but also behave like it.

> *Even if you have no idea what trout are feeding on when you're on the water, if you know what naturals are generally available you can try the most likely imitations until the right one is found. This improves the chances of catching fish enormously over the method of using any old fly and just hoping.*

The physical factors to take into consideration when choosing a fly are size, shape and colour. The factors for consideration when trying to mimic behaviour are action, place and time.

The first three factors are fairly obvious and are covered by picking a fly from the box that is roughly the right shape, approximately the same colour, and as close as possible in size to the natural being imitated. The behavioural factors are more demanding of the angler.

Action

Action relates to the movement of the natural in the water. This may simply be lying on the bottom or drifting with the current, or it could be actively swimming against the current, across the surface or towards the bottom. Unnatural behaviour will usually stop a trout taking an artificial fly.

Many of the creatures that form part of the trout's diet drift with the current in flowing water but when they have to swim, whether in stillwater or flowing water, they move at a pace relative to their size.

CHOOSING THE RIGHT FLY

In real terms small creatures move slowly and larger creatures move relatively faster and this should be borne in mind when retrieving.

Place

Place can relate to the position of the fly in the column of water or to a particular spot on the river or lake. The position of the fly in the river column can be on or close to the bottom; mid water; immediately beneath the surface; in the surface film; or floating on the surface. The variance between the latter three can be a matter of a few millimetres, but can mean the difference between catching lots of fish or none at all.

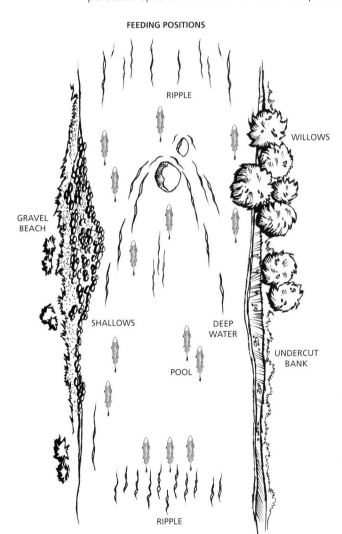

In rivers trout rarely feed mid water when it is more than half a metre deep, so in running water we need the fly to be close to the bottom or near the top. In stillwaters trout will feed at any depth but more often near the bottom or right on top.

CONTINUES PAGE 46

CHOOSING THE RIGHT FLY

SAMPLE FLY SELECTION

This selection of flies is far from exhaustive, but is a good starting point. No doubt you will soon acquire many more for your fly box.

VARIOUS STAGES OF THE INSECT'S LIFE CYCLE →

Natural	mayfly nymph	dun	spinner
Imitation	**hare's ear**	**adams**	**adams**
Natural	cased caddis	sedge pupa	adult sedge
Imitation	**woolly caddis**	**bead head hare's ear**	**deer hair sedge**
Natural	bloodworm	midge pupa	adult midge
Imitation	**bloodworm**	**midge pupa/buzzer**	**adams**
Natural	waterboatman		
Imitation	**corixa**		
Natural	damsel nymph	damselfly	
Imitation	**marabou damsel**	**damselfly**	
Natural	brown beetle	green beetle	
Imitation	**coch-y-bondhu**	**coch-y-bondhu**	
Natural	Bully	whitebait	smelt
Imitation	**Mrs Simpson**	**Jack's sprat**	**grey ghost**
Natural	snail		
Imitation	**black and peacock**		

CHOOSING THE RIGHT FLY

CHOOSING THE RIGHT FLY

POSITION OF FLY ON THE WATER COLUMN

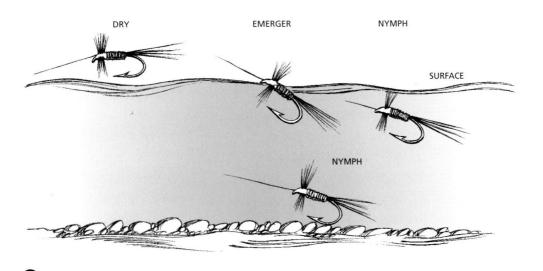

The feeding position in a pool or lake will be covered in the later chapters on fishing streams, rivers and stillwaters.

Time

Time might seem an odd factor to consider. After all, we know the right time to use a particular imitation when we can see trout taking the corresponding natural. But what about those instances when we have to guess what trout are feeding on because we can't see the natural or the trout (or both)? On these occasions knowledge of the natural's life cycle and activities can help prevent a poor choice of imitation. For instance, if you can see trout rising in the middle of a hot, sunny summer's day, but you can't see what they are taking, tying on an adult sedge imitation would not be a good idea, as these insects hatch in the failing light of evening and not in full sunlight. Equally, fishing a cicada pattern on a high country lake in the early spring would be inappropriate, as cicadas wouldn't appear on the water till after Christmas.

Most of the time trout are opportunistic feeders; if any sort of food comes along they will take it. This means that if you fish a fly that represents something they are used to eating, you will have a chance of catching trout. However, there are occasions when there is such an abundance of a particular item of food, trout will become preoccupied with it and ignore everything else. In fly fishing terms this is called selective feeding. We read a lot about this in fly fishing literature, but it is the exception rather than the rule. Nonetheless, it pays to be aware of it so that it can be recognized and dealt with. Most of the time we don't need to have all six factors (size, shape, colour, action, place and time) covered. Often four will produce a few fish, but when trout are being selective all six are a must to ensure consistent success.

There are occasions when trout can be caught on fly when they are not feeding. This is done by playing on their territorial instinct. It is not uncommon to see trout chasing off smaller fish that get too near them. It is also easy to catch trout that are spawning – just cast a large lure pattern near them. They will see it as a threat to their eggs and attack it.

In the tributaries of Lake Taupo and the Rotorua lakes it is not so much the pattern of fly that is important there but the way that it is fished. It must be at the right depth and fished close to the fish that are resting on their upstream migration. Fly colour can be important as this affects the visibility of the fly according to the light and the clarity of the water.

Fishing
streams & rivers

In previous chapters we have seen how trout behave and what they feed on. Now we need to look at how we use the fly we have chosen to deceive the trout. First of all we need to decide whether we are going to cast upstream or downstream. The type of fly that we have tied on will largely determine this. If our choice of fly requires a drag-free drift to imitate an insect that is being carried along by the current, then we need to cast upstream. If we need the fly to swing across the current (such as when fishing a feathered lure to imitate a small fish), then we will cast downstream.

Most of the time when we are imitating insects that trout feed on we would use a floating line and this is assumed throughout this chapter unless stated otherwise.

All this begs the basic question – how do we decide what fly should be tied on? This is the crux of fly fishing, in that once we know what fly to tie on, everything else is relatively simple.

If trout can be seen rising and we can see what they are rising to, it is easy to pick a suitable imitation from the fly box and fish it in an appropriate manner as described in the previous chapter.

Things are a little more difficult if we can see fish feeding either from the surface or beneath the surface but we can't see what it is that they are taking. If the trout are not breaking the surface we need to fish a sunk fly beneath the surface; if they are breaking the surface we need to fish a fly on the surface. However, trout sometimes feed beneath the surface but so close to it that their dorsal fins or tails break the surface and it is easy to mistake this for a rise to a surface fly. If there are bubbles in the rings of a rise, the chances are the fish is feeding from the surface. Another clue is that there is usually noise when trout surface feed, whereas a subsurface rise is silent.

When casting to feeding trout that can be seen it is better to cast at an angle than from directly downstream, as the chances of hooking the fish are better. When casting from behind it is not unusual for the nose of the trout to bump the tippet, which prevents it getting the fly into its mouth. At an angle the tippet easily goes into the mouth and the hook usually finds a hold in the corner of the jaw.

The crunch comes when there are no trout rising and nothing obvious for trout to feed on. This scenario, despite what we read in articles and books on fly fishing, is the most common you will encounter. Because it is so common we need a sound strategy to deal with the situation.

BEST ANGLE TO FISH

ANGLER

There is one thing that is definite – as there is nothing to be seen, the trout are feeding subsurface and probably down deep. Since we know that trout rarely feed midwater, we need to get the fly close to the bottom. If the water is more than half a metre deep, the fly will need to be weighted to get there. The creatures that trout will be feeding on close to the bottom will be brownish or greenish in colour and will be drifting drag-free, that is, being carried along freely with the current.

We now know what to do. Firstly, cast upstream in the ripples on a shortish line, about 5 or 6 metres. As the nymph drifts downstream, gather the line in with the line hand, to keep slack to a minimum. A close watch is kept on the end of the fly line or strike indicator. If the end of the line stops or pulls under, or the indicator disappears, lift the rod tip immediately in case a trout has taken the nymph. It could be just hooked up on the bottom, but don't take chances; always assume it is a fish. If you don't lift the rod tip and it is a fish, the chances of hooking it are greatly reduced.

Cover as much water as possible in this manner, remembering that you are trying to get the fly near the bottom. Having the fly whipping downstream in the current a metre or more above the river bed is not going to be productive. Cover the water systematically: don't cast at random. Make the first cast close to the bank, then the next a metre or so further out, and so on until you have covered as much water as possible. Then take a couple of steps upstream and repeat the process. This way of fishing can be a bit monotonous, but it can often produce the odd fish when nothing else will. On a good day results can be spectacular.

> *A habit that many beginners get into, and some more experienced fishers too, is that of standing in one place and repeatedly covering the same patch of water. Unless you are doing something different every few casts, this is a total waste of time. If you are fishing the correct fly and covering the water properly any fish present will take in the first 2 or 3 casts. If there is no response in that time, move on.*

If you hook a fish lead it away from the area so that it doesn't spook any others that are present. The trout was there because it was a good place to feed, so there could well be others. When hooked in ripples trout usually run downstream and towards the middle and the depths of the pool. Let them go there and play them out before landing them and returning to fish the ripple again. In well populated waters there may be lots of fish in ripples at times. This won't happen often, so make the most of every opportunity.

The same method can be used when fishing flat water, but demands greater concentration. When there are terrestrials about, the water can be explored with a dry fly instead of a nymph. This requires less concentration as takes are more obvious.

> There are lots of places that fish can hide and it pays to fish all the likely places, even if we can't see fish. It is always worth trying in the shadows beneath trees, in ripples, along undercut banks and alongside weedbeds.

A hot spot on the Waipahi River.

Fishing a feathered lure on a sunk line is sometimes looked down upon by so called 'nymph fishers', but fishing the feathered lure correctly demands concentration and skill. On big waters a long cast is needed and control of the line is required to move it slowly through likely lies. The line needs to be mended (see illustration), which means throwing loops of slack line upstream to get the fly down deep and prevent it from dragging rapidly across the current.

MENDING THE LINE
SLOW WATER
FAST WATER
ANGLER

Good knowledge of where fish lie when migrating upstream is a must if we are to be consistently successful. One area where fish like to lie is just off the main current to one side or the other, or just where the current flattens out in the main part of the pool. In many waters there are lies that produce fish year after year; these need to be learned.

Fishing *Stillwaters*

Many fly fishers never come to grips with stillwater fly fishing, which is a shame as they are missing some great fishing. Stillwaters range in size from small ponds to Lake Taupo.

At the larger end of the scale stillwaters can be intimidating because of their sheer size. Even a long cast seems to make little impression on the vast expanse of water. The temptation in this situation is to wade out as far as possible and then cast as far as possible, but this is a big mistake. Most trout food is produced around the margins of stillwaters – consequently, trout will often be found feeding in very shallow water indeed. Sometimes there will be barely enough water to cover a fish's back.

FISHING STILLWATERS

> *When approaching the water always start looking for fish well before you get to the water's edge. It is a waste of an opportunity to scare fish from the shallows when they can be caught with just a short cast.*

One aspect of stillwater fishing is the apparent featurelessness of the water. It is not always obvious where trout can be found. Despite the fact that stillwater trout are continually on the move when feeding, there are certain places that will be more productive than others.

The spot where a stream flows into a lake is usually worth fishing. Some of the classic fishing spots in New Zealand are at the mouths of Taupo tributaries. Weedbeds are always worth a look for trout patrolling their edges in search of food. Silty shallows are worth a go early in the morning or at dusk, as they often produce good hatches of midge. An offshore wind from tussock or bush can bring trout in close to feed on terrestrials blown onto the water. Rushes growing in the water can be productive when damselflies or dragonflies are hatching, as the nymphs migrate towards them and use them to crawl out of the water. The shade of trees and bushes in sunny weather can be worth a cast with a terrestrial pattern.

In man-made lakes there will be old river channels running out from the bank. Trout like to cruise these channels as the depth gives them security. In these man-made waters there is ready access to deep water by fishing off the dam, especially when the margins are too warm for trout.

Lastly the outlet of lakes can be very productive. Unfortunately many of them have control structures in place, but the few remaining natural outlets provide great fishing.

Another problem that has to be dealt with when fishing stillwaters is where to cast when a trout rises. Obviously the fly must be cast in front

Fishing the shallows of a stillwater.

of the fish, but it is not always easy to tell which way it is swimming. Trout invariably feed upwind so if you see a rise, cast a couple of metres upwind and a couple of metres beyond the rise. Retrieve the fly as soon as it hits the water and expect a take at any time.

If it is calm it can be a bit more difficult, but trout often feed parallel to the shore rather than in and out when it is calm, so cast to the right and then, if there is no response on the first cast, try casting to the left. Ten seconds is long enough to leave the fly in the water before recasting.

Fishing blind can be very productive in stillwaters. Trout still have to feed, and even if there is nothing on the surface, there is always plenty of food down below. The most efficient way to cover the water is to cast across the wind and then retrieve the fly. The path of the fly describes an arc and covers a lot of water, potentially crossing the path of any passing trout.

FISHING STILLWATERS

When trout are feeding on surface food such as cicadas, beetles or damselflies, it pays just to cast your fly out in the vicinity of rising trout, leave it there and wait for a fish to take it. When fishing a sedge it is worth retrieving it slowly to reproduce the wake of the natural running across the water. When striking with a dry fly on stillwater it pays to do so slowly. This is true on running water too, but on stillwater when you see the fish break the surface, give it plenty of time to turn down and close its mouth before you lift to set the hook.

Fishing stillwaters may not be your cup of tea, but often when rivers are unfishable due to high water a stillwater can be found somewhere that is fishable.

A good take.

Learning Tips

The best way to learn to fish is just to get out there and do it, but there are several ways to speed up the learning process. Firstly it is a good idea to pick a water to fish regularly, and not just any old water but one that holds enough fish to make it interesting and isn't too far away from home. Fishing a water regularly helps you to see the patterns of fish behaviour both on a daily basis and throughout a season. If you fish a lot of waters and they are all different in character it will be difficult to see a pattern emerging.

Read books on fly fishing. Since you are reading this you have already made a start, but remember that just because something is in print it isn't necessarily true – read critically. The same applies when talking to other fly fishers. Anglers are always keen to pass on advice, but be sure to check the credentials of anyone offering it to you. You may find they know less than yourself.

LEARNING TIPS

Keep a fishing diary – anything you read in it should be true! It pays to read over your diary to see if any pattern emerges, especially at the end of the season. When you have kept a diary for several seasons it is good to read up all the entries for the water to be fished on the next outing, as it may remind you of something that will help catch a few more fish. Diaries are a great check for the memory; anglers' memories are notoriously unreliable. Fooling yourself will not increase your catch rate.

This little book has just scratched the surface of fly fishing, but will hopefully point you in the right direction. Be warned… once you get started, you could find yourself on the slippery slope to a lifetime of fly fishing.

> *One thing to remember – the trout call the shots and if you ever start to think that it's not fair, then you've lost the plot.*

A fishing diary can prove very useful to the committed angler. Photocopy the page opposite and you will be able to keep an accurate record of all your future fly fishing expeditions.

FISHING DIARY

DATE: January 3rd

LOCATION: Waitaki River

FISH / WEIGHT: 2x Rainbow trout
First one was 1.5kg
Second one was 1kg

FLY USED: Deer hair sedge

COMMENTS: Warm, calm evening after a hot day. Right on dusk trout rising everywhere to a big hatch of sedges.

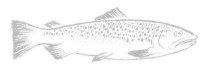

FISHING DIARY

DATE:

LOCATION:

FISH / WEIGHT:

FLY USED:

COMMENTS: